Prais

Any praying parent has times when she simply doesn't know how to pray for her child or when she finds it difficult to pray at all. On top of this, we are often pulled in multiple directions to care for the emotional, physical, mental, and spiritual development of our children. We rush to sports practice, then a music recital, then dinner and bedtime. It can be tough to pause and intentionally pray for our children prayers that align with the concerns of God laid out in his Word. This is where Kathleen's prayers come alongside us in our weariness, anxiety, and ambitions. These prayers are worth sitting with, chewing on, and praying. I will be using and sharing this resource for many years to come.

—**Quina Aragon**, Author, *Love Made: A Story of God's Overflowing, Creative Heart* and *Love Gave: A Story of God's Greatest Gift*

If you, like the Hugheses, have sometimes longed for words adequate to express your heart's prayers for your growing children—and wished for more—Kathleen Nielson's *Prayers of a Parent for Young Children* is for you. The book features thirty-one select Bible texts, each accompanied by an expository note that is then paired with an exquisite prayer-poem. And because poetic expression (with its "rhythms, sounds, and meanings") naturally lodges in our minds and elevates our thoughts—especially when it is based on sacred Scripture—it enlarges our vocabulary for prayer. This book is a wonderful gift to both parent and child. Highly recommended!

—**Kent and Barbara Hughes**, Authors; Speakers; Longtime Pastor and Pastor's Wife

Praise for the Prayers of a Parent Series

We love how these beautiful, biblical prayers help us to "pray most earnestly" (1 Thess. 3:10), to "pray without ceasing"

(1 Thess. 5:17), and to pray specifically for our own children. Furthermore, pastors should encourage every member to pray for the children of the church and assist them in doing so. This book would be a huge help to that end, for often people are willing to pray but "do not know what to pray for" (Rom. 8:26). For those in congregations that take vows to assist parents in the Christian nurture of their children, we can't imagine a better or more important way of fulfilling their vows than praying for those children from their youth onward.

—**Anne and Ligon Duncan**, Wife, Mother, Christian Educator; Chancellor and CEO, Reformed Theological Seminary

I know of no greater gift that a parent can give to their child than the gift of prayer centered on the gospel. That's why I'm so excited about this project from Kathleen Nielson. Filled with faith, hope, and love, each prayer is accompanied by relevant Scripture and a focused exhortation to help any parent put into words what they long for in their hearts. Having prayed for and with our two daughters for the last two decades, my wife and I look forward to using it!

—**Julius J. Kim**, President, The Gospel Coalition

Kathleen Nielson has coupled scriptural truth with beautifully crafted poetic prayers that bring hope. As a mom, I am encouraged to consider afresh the many ways I must pray for my children. Kathleen helps me with the joyful task by lifting my eyes upward, creating a Word-focused mission of intercession. As a parent (whether natural or spiritual), you too will be challenged in the prayers you pray—prayers that are bound to change not only your children's hearts but yours as well.

—**Blair Linne**, Author; Speaker; Spoken Word Artist

Kathleen Nielson understands the longings of our hearts for the spiritual flourishing of our children. She gives these longings beautiful and Bible-shaped expression. A treasure for every Christian parent!

—**Dane C. Ortlund**, Author, *Gentle and Lowly: The Heart of Christ for Sinners and Sufferers*

There is no greater joy for Christian parents than to hear that their children are walking in the truth. But how do we pray toward that end, day in and day out, through every stage of their lives? I can think of no better guide than this series by Kathleen Nielson—a diligent student of God's Word, a wonderful writer, and a praying mother (and now grandmother). Because these prayers are so Scripture saturated, you can have confidence that you are praying in accord with the will of our good and sovereign God. Take up and read, and pray, and by God's grace you could change your world.

—**Justin Taylor**, Managing Editor, *ESV Study Bible*

Since as parents we have no ability whatsoever to change the hearts of our children, prayer for them is not a spiritual luxury; it is essential. It is an amazing grace to us that God welcomes, hears, and answers our prayers. I know of no other guide to parental prayer like Nielson's tender, insightful, gospel-rich, and loving little book. Read it and you will find yourself praying for new things for your children in new ways than you have before, and as you do, you will grow in affection for your Father and in how you approach him in prayer.

—**Paul David Tripp**, Author, *New Morning Mercies: A Daily Gospel Devotional* and *Parenting: 14 Gospel Principles That Can Radically Change Your Family*

Parenting is important and hard. How do you pray through this complexity? What do you pray when you aren't sure what to say or how to say it? Kathleen Nielson knows the parental spiritual roller-coaster. She's lived it. And prayed through it.

This book will give you words to pray and encouragement to ponder as you navigate the issues and challenges of real-world parenting. It helped me. I think it will help you as well.

—**Mark Vroegop**, Lead Pastor, College Park Church, Indianapolis; Author, *Dark Clouds, Deep Mercy: Discovering the Grace of Lament*

Prayers of a Parent
for Young Children

Prayers of a Parent Series

KATHLEEN NIELSON

Prayers of a Parent for Young Children
Prayers of a Parent for Teens
Prayers of a Parent for Young Adults
Prayers of a Parent for Adult Children

Prayers of a Parent
for Young Children

Kathleen Nielson

P U B L I S H I N G
P.O. BOX 817 • PHILLIPSBURG • NEW JERSEY 08865-0817

Scripture quotations are from the ESV® Bible (The Holy Bible, English Standard Version®), copyright © 2001 by Crossway, a publishing ministry of Good News Publishers. Used by permission. All rights reserved.

Italics within Scripture quotations indicate emphasis added.

Printed in the United States of America

Library of Congress Cataloging-in-Publication Data

Names: Nielson, Kathleen Buswell, author.
Title: Prayers of a parent for young children / Kathleen Nielson.
Description: Phillipsburg, New Jersey : P&R Publishing, [2021] | Series: Prayers of a parent | Summary: "Poetic prayers address the spiritual well-being, physical needs, and character growth of a child from infancy to preteen years. They are accompanied by brief reflections and Scripture passages for meditation"-- Provided by publisher.
Identifiers: LCCN 2021008072 | ISBN 9781629958170 (paperback) | ISBN 9781629958187 (epub) | ISBN 9781629958194 (mobi)
Subjects: LCSH: Parents--Prayers and devotions. | Children--Prayers and devotions. | Children--Religious life. | Parent and child--Religious aspects--Christianity.
Classification: LCC BV4529 .N544 2021 | DDC 242/.645--dc23
LC record available at https://lccn.loc.gov/2021008072

For our three sons,
and their three beautiful wives, now like daughters,
and our grandchildren, eight so far—
what amazing gifts from God.
I love praying for you!

Contents

Contents

Introduction

How being a parent makes one pray! And how amazing to think that Christian parents can reach out in prayer to God our Father, who has shown his love to us in his own Son—and who gives us his Holy Spirit to help us pray, according to his Word.

These prayers have grown from my heart through years of praying for three sons—and now for their growing families. I know that you parents (and grandparents, and aunts and uncles, and spiritual mothers and fathers!) will surely pray for your children in your own words and with your own specific praises and petitions. My hope is that these prayers might mingle profitably with yours, as we all lift up the next generations to the Lord who knows and loves them perfectly.

These prayers grow out of the Scriptures; each is printed with a brief related Bible passage and reflects that passage in its content. What confidence, that when we don't know how to pray for our children, the Spirit and the Word guide and help us. Just as the Scriptures show us Jesus Christ at the very center, so these prayers aim to focus on Jesus—his love, his work of salvation on our behalf, his glory, his blessed rule in every area of our lives, his coming again.

The prayers apply to sons and daughters both; they alternate, but any of them can easily be changed by switching the pronouns appropriately. Please note as well that the prayers are written in one parent's voice, although they can certainly be prayed by parents together.

This volume offers prayers for young children, from birth through the preteen years. Parents, please know that these prayers, as they focus on our children, inevitably focus often on us parents too. Prayer stretches our hearts in all kinds of ways.

Let us pray!

Kathleen Nielson

As you do not know the way the spirit comes to the bones in the womb of a woman with child, so you do not know the work of God who makes everything. (Eccl. 11:5)

Here is where we must begin, with eyes to see a child as a glorious creation of our God who made the world and everything in it.

It stretches our souls to imagine the Lord God in the beginning creating the heavens and the earth. And it stretches our souls to imagine the Lord God creating a new, unique human being within a woman's body.

We cannot understand, but we wonder at "the work of God who makes everything."

Second stanza (*O Jesus Christ our Lord*): see John 1:1–3, 14.

Of Worship to the Lord of Life

O Father God in heaven,
you are life within yourself;
all your creation holds together
only by your word.

O Jesus Christ our Lord,
the Word made flesh, the One
by whom and for whom all was made,
we worship at your feet.

O Spirit of the risen Christ,
the One who breathes the Word
and breathes life into bones,
we joy to feel your breath.

All praise to you, Lord God,
Creator of vast planets,
myriad stars, and a tiny child
within a woman's womb.

Behold, children are a heritage from the LORD. *(Ps. 127:3)*

A child is not something of our own or of our own doing; a child is a gift from the Lord—a "heritage" (an inheritance) given that we might know and pass on the treasures of his name, generation by generation.

Receiving this gift, we must first express our thanksgiving to the Giver. First and always, may we look up and thank our gracious God for such a gift.

Of Thanksgiving
for the Gift of a Child

It is the ultimately humble prayer, O Lord,
I offer up to you,
I who can work and make so many things
but who cannot create a human life.

I bow before the One who makes
and gives and takes the gift of life,
with thankfulness I scarce know how to speak,
knowing the greatness and the mystery of the gift.

In steadfast love and faithfulness
from heaven long ago you planned this life,
designed it in your image
as a heritage from you,
given to carry on your name.

My gracious Father, let me not forget
to pour out lifelong thanks to you
the way I do this moment full
of wonder at the child
you've let me cradle in my arms.

For God so loved the world, that he gave his only Son, that whoever believes in him should not perish but have eternal life. (John 3:16)

The church my family attended during my growing-up years had John 3:16 (in the beautiful old King James Version) engraved in large gilded letters framed in white and centered on the front wall of the sanctuary for all to see.

That verse is engraved on my childhood memories—and, by God's grace, on my heart. There it is, the universe-changing truth, the truth we pray will be engraved on our children's hearts: God so loved the world that he gave his Son.

All the rest of the prayers offered in this book build on this foundational prayer: that our sons and daughters might be reconciled to God through faith in Christ and become eternally part of God's family.

We cannot know the ways in which the Lord will answer. But we can know the goodness of this prayer, offered only for the glory of the Lord Jesus.

Like the invisible wind: see John 3:1–15.

For the Gift of Eternal Life

How you give the gift of life that never ends—
as Nicodemus learned—
is full of mystery,
like the invisible wind that blows
and bends the branches as it will.

For this child I pray your Spirit's breath
will bend his mind and heart toward you, Lord God,
that as he hears of Jesus and his love,
his death in our poor place,
his resurrection from the grave,
early this child may believe
that Jesus is the Christ,
your Son who died to save,
the risen Lord who lives to intercede
for him.

Many petitions I would make,
O loving Father;
this one remains all for now
and all for ever. Would you,
by your grace,
bend down to give my child
the gift of eternal life?

Lead me in the path of your commandments,
for I delight in it. (Ps. 119:35)

With a child, we have the amazing chance to share the Bible's living words not as rote truth to be transferred—but with delight, as we get to help them hear our heavenly Father's voice speaking to us.

With a child, we can be amazed all over again that Scripture's words are breathed out by God, that they are able to make us "wise for salvation," that they are "profitable for teaching, for reproof, for correction, and for training in righteousness" (2 Tim. 3:15–16).

We will speak so many words to our children day by day as they grow. Our own words will not be perfect; in fact, they will often seem inadequate. What a joy to know that we can give them God's Word—perfect, beautiful, and true.

While sitting in our house: see Deuteronomy 6:4–9. *The Word made flesh:* see John 1:1–14.

For Love of God's Word

You made us creatures of words, Lord God,
like you our Maker;
so we hear and understand and speak—
because you do.

I pray my child will take delight in words,
and most of all the words breathed out by you,
so mercifully given in your Holy Word.
Help me to carry your Word deep,
with stores that purify and sweeten
my words' flow—while sitting in our house,
or walking by the way, or lying down, or rising.
May I teach your Scriptures well,
and joyfully, in harmony
with voices of your people all around.

May scenes and stories capture her,
the poetry enliven her imaginings,
the teachings take firm root
and bear good fruit, in every season.

May she love your Word,
and love the Word made flesh,
the Savior who shines forth
on every page.

O Lord, how manifold are your works!
In wisdom have you made them all;
the earth is full of your creatures. (Ps. 104:24)

We're all so busy! A parent of young children vividly knows the reality of many cares and responsibilities to fit into a day (and sometimes a night as well).

In the midst of all our pressing things, however, surely one of the gifts wrapped up in a child is the gift of having to stop so often—whether it be stopping to rock and feed a baby or, later, stopping on a walk to see a bird or an airplane in the sky or the roly-polies on the sidewalk. I have a granddaughter who loves to collect roly-polies and to see how each of these crunchy little bugs curls up into a little ball when you touch it. This takes time.

It is good time! It is God-given time. It is time that helps us to see everything else with clearer eyes and soul.

For Joy in God's Creation

For roly-polies on the sidewalk
give me time, O Lord,
for you made all the bugs, and butterflies,
and birds appearing like paint streaks on canvas
or like an intricately patterned sketch,
should one bird perch and show himself—
and should we stop and see.

Please let me learn from a child's eyes
the glory of the greening grass,
surprising sharpness of the blades
against a tender hand,
the mystery of a budding branch
that looks dry, dark and dead,
but hides a promise
in the color folded tight
until the sun's hand reaches down
and coaxes, woos buds open with its warmth.

So work in my beloved child (also in me), Creator God.
Reach down and open wide and wider yet
our eyes and, yes, our souls.
Cause us to pause, in days of childhood chances;
distract us with delight to see your works
and in them find your wisdom overflowing
through the manifold witness of the world you made.

For roly-polies on the sidewalk
give me time, O Lord . . .

For you formed my inward parts;
*   you knitted me together in my mother's womb.*
I praise you, for I am fearfully and wonderfully made.
Wonderful are your works;
*   my soul knows it very well. (Ps. 139:13–14)*

The years of parenting a baby and then a young child are necessarily years of focusing on the child's body—as we care for their bathing, eating, sleeping, growing, learning to walk and talk, and on and on.

Clearly, our Creator God from the beginning intended that we human beings should be creatures alive in body and soul. What a comfort that our bodies are important to God! He knits together each human body from its very conception in the womb.

Even as we care lovingly for our children's bodies, this prayer asks our heavenly Father to help us all know and trust his care for each one of us his children, body and soul, to the end.

For My Child's Body

Protect this child's body you have made, O loving Lord
(in my protecting, let me trust your hand).

Watch over breathing lungs and beating heart
(in my night watch, let me not fail to wonder
at the parts all knit together by your unerring hand).

So helpless born, please let him grow to find his help in you
(in my caregiving, Lord, remind me of my need
met by your all-sufficient hand).

Please give him health and growth, sweet sleep, and appetite
(in my providing, may I rest assured
in the provision of your sovereign hand).

When sickness comes, may you bring comfort, healing
(in my doubt or worry, Father, teach me
how to give my child into your loving hand).

Lead him to thank you for the body knit for him
(help me light up your good design for humans
male and female, in your image, showing the Creator's hand).

Lead him to praise you,
knowing he is fearfully and wonderfully made
(and let the praise that rises from our home
grow into wonder at the One who took on flesh
to save us fleshly creatures, by his redeeming hand).

As you come to him, a living stone rejected by men but in the sight of God chosen and precious, you yourselves like living stones are being built up as a spiritual house, to be a holy priesthood, to offer spiritual sacrifices acceptable to God through Jesus Christ. (1 Peter 2:4–5)

The child of a believer right away has a place in the family of God—the church. As Christians, our fundamental and eternal identity is in Christ as part of his body; how crucial it is for our children early on to come to know (and, we pray, to join by faith) our forever family. We should not underestimate the way a child is shaped and drawn in the earliest years, and we should especially not underestimate the importance of the church from the start.

None of us is meant to raise our children all by ourselves; we need the wisdom and the encouragement of others in our family—especially the family of believers. And our church family needs the children. Believers young and old, in all life's contexts, help to hold and teach and love the children and find joy in doing so.

For Love of the Church

Let her know a host of loving arms, Lord God,
and voices young and ancient, deep and high,
all lifted up in singing and in prayer,
in laughter large and weeping shared.

Let her sense silence and the Spirit's breath
when Word is read and preached
and sent like arrows into hearts
to comfort, or to pierce and purify our thoughts.

Let her love family both near and far;
may she not fear to welcome a new sister,
hold the hand of aunt or uncle in the faith,
and listen well to wisdom from more mouths than mine.

May she know Jesus not just from the Word
taught and by grace lived out at home,
but may she hear and see and love him
in the house of faith where saints are living stones.

In peace I will both lie down and sleep;
for you alone, O LORD, make me dwell in safety. (Ps. 4:8)

Endless theories and articles are out there on the subject of how best to help your child (and you) get a good night's sleep. Some of them are good.

We can pray about this! We should pray about this—and what a help to pray and to meditate on Scripture's words concerning day and night, and rest, and even peaceful sleep.

For Sleep

I know that we will need no sleep
when finally we get to where there is no night,
no sin, no end to light . . .

But now, Lord God, you made us
creatures of the night and day.
We know the love of light,
and we soon learn the need for rest by night,
when sun is gone from sight
and moon rules in its place,
marking seasons with its sometimes plumpness,
sometimes tantalizing fingernail of light.

As night by night the moon takes up its watch,
let my child sleep
in safety and in peace,
O Lord who rules both day and night.
Let him sleep deep.
Let him learn rest
that one day will provide for him
a picture of his rest in you,
all through the love of Christ.
Let him learn trust in you who never sleep,
who watch your children with unceasing love
through all the span of nights and days
you've measured out for us,
until the Day we wake and see your face.

Children, obey your parents in everything, for this pleases the Lord. Fathers, do not provoke your children, lest they become discouraged. (Col. 3:20–21)

If we weren't sinful parents teaching obedience to sinful children, it would be so much easier.

We can never do this by ourselves. And we are not called to. Only by God's grace, through the power of Christ our risen Savior, are sinful hearts softened and changed—both ours and those of our children.

By God's grace, he uses us parents to teach our children how to obey . . . how to repent when we fail . . . how to find forgiveness . . . how to persevere. We do this depending on God's Word, strengthened by God's Spirit, encouraged by God's people around us—and praying day by day.

For Obedience

I pray for open ears
in my beloved sinful child—
and, from my mouth, words wise and clear.

I pray, Lord, for your Spirit's work
to soften her heart at the point of choice—
and, for my part, a godly life that lights the way.

I pray for her repentance when she fails,
a soul wide open to forgiveness—
and, from my heart, like yours, a ready store.

I pray for discipline to grow within her,
habits of heeding your Word's call—
and, as I guide, unfailing gentleness and strength from you.

I pray for her to seek the Savior,
righteous one who showed obedience full and true—
and, as I point to Jesus, let me show his life in me.

I pray that she would learn the happiness
of one who trusts and who obeys—
and, leading, may I show how good are your commands.

A friend loves at all times,
    and a brother is born for adversity. (Prov. 17:17)

From the earliest days of babyhood through all the different stages of growth, children's friends help to shape their view of the world and their sense of their own place in it. We grow in understanding through relationships with others—ultimately with God, through Jesus the friend to sinners. But God made us to learn and grow through the gift of the people around us.

At first, we parents get to be our children's best friends, and that is good . . . for a while. We can pray for and help them to discover friends God puts in their paths, ones who can help teach them about loving and being loved.

What a gift—a childhood friend!

To walk the paths of wisdom: see Proverbs 4:18–27. The entirety of Proverbs 4 is great fodder for prayer.

For Friendships

There is no perfect friend but you, dear Lord,
but would you send some friends like you
to walk the paths of wisdom with my child
and help him keep his gaze full straight ahead,
not swerving to the right or left,
but urging one another on toward light?

And would you make him such a friend to others,
one who loves no matter what—
sharing what he'd like to keep,
forgiving what he might begrudge,
holding a tongue that would speak harm,
showing mercy where the world might mock?

I pray for friendships in God's family
that give my child a taste of heaven,
and friendships in the world
that give him ways to share that taste.

And may he come to treasure
the true Friend of sinners who came down
and loved and saved us needy ones
who marvel we can call him friend.

Rejoice always, pray without ceasing, give thanks in all cir-cumstances; for this is the will of God in Christ Jesus for you. (1 Thess. 5:16–18)

You may or may not carry with you the examples of parents who lived lives full of prayer and who shared prayer with their children. No parent does this perfectly. But what a heritage to aim for and to *pray* for: a heritage of prayer, the passed-on habit of talking to God our Father, in the name of Jesus Christ our Lord.

We will inevitably pass on lots of habits to our children—the ways we fold our clothes, cook our eggs, cross our legs! May we consider well the spiritual disciplines that we have the chance to pass on to our children—especially the habit of prayer.

For a Heart to Pray

I thank you that you hear your children when they pray,
O gracious Father in heaven.
Amazing grace—that you should make a way
for us to come unhindered, bold,
in Jesus's name and washed clean by his blood.

Help me to practice prayer
both in my closet shut away
and with my child—
at table, bedside, riding in the car,
in sudden griefs both large and small,
in joys for which we regularly fail
to give you thanks.

Merciful Father, teach me the privilege of prayer;
make me a teacher who is ever learning;
make my child, by your amazing grace,
a child of yours who learns and loves
to lift up words of prayer to you our Father in heaven.

Whoever despises his neighbor is a sinner,
  but blessed is he who is generous to the poor. (Prov. 14:21)

These prayers for our children certainly become convicting to us!

We all know that generosity is not an automatic instinct in us sinful human beings. Children learn early how to say "Mine!" Children also offer us parents some of the most challenging opportunities to give up things like time and space that we previously held sacred for ourselves, in order to give our children what they need.

Children provide a wonderful catalyst for the cultivation of all kinds of generosity. In neighborhoods and churches and schools, through our children we connect with other families who will need our help, even as we may need theirs. We can pray to see with God's eyes and respond with open hearts to needs both big and little, inside and outside our homes.

In the midst of whatever need or plenty God ordains, how good for us to pray to learn and teach the blessing of generosity that God first taught to us in the giving of his own Son.

For Generosity

However poor or rich we find ourselves,
O God who gave your Son
to save us poor and needy sinners,
teach poor me, and teach my child through me,
how to be the neighbor rich in generosity
to those less full and fortunate.
Let us share food, or money,
time to listen,
time to help,
and time to learn
from those who suffer need.

Please give my child an open heart
and open eyes to see the needs around her,
not considering herself the answer or the source,
but humbly serving you who give us all we have
and spreading the provision flowing from your hand.

From toys tight-held, to entertainment counted on,
to space that's *mine*, to all that's *mine*,
release her grip, Lord. Release *mine*.
Teach us the blessing of a generous heart.

But let all who take refuge in you rejoice;
  let them ever sing for joy,
and spread your protection over them,
  that those who love your name may exult in you.
    (Ps. 5:11)

We want joy for our children. We long for joyful homes, joyful days—joyful lives as they unfold.

How do we aim for and pray for joy? The more we read Scripture, the more it looks like joy is not a thing in itself to seek but rather the overflow of relationship with God, who is the source of true and lasting joy.

In the midst of happy and sad childhood days, we can pray for this kind of joy for our children (and for ourselves)—joy in the Lord himself.

For Joy

Let my child live in joy;
Lord, fill our home with light through windows,
light in eyes,
light souls, not weighed down with sin,
all through the cleansing blood of Jesus.
So, what I pray is this:
please let my child find life in you, O loving Lord.

May my child be quick to laugh
the deep-down laughter
rising from a fearless soul
that revels in divine protection,
which I pray you would spread over us
to cover happiness and sorrow alike.
May my beloved child take refuge and rejoice
in you, Lord God.

Please let my child's song be joy
in little moments now,
and all the ones to come;
may neither happiness nor trouble
silence his soul's song of praise to you.
So, what I pray is this, my Father God:
please let him learn to love your name,
exult in you,
and sing for joy.

Besides being wise, the Preacher also taught the people knowledge, weighing and studying and arranging many proverbs with great care. The Preacher sought to find words of delight, and uprightly he wrote words of truth.

The words of the wise are like goads, and like nails firmly fixed are the collected sayings; they are given by one Shepherd. My son, beware of anything beyond these. Of making many books there is no end, and much study is a weariness of the flesh. (Eccl. 12:9–12)

I love the way the writer of Ecclesiastes describes his inspired writing process as crafting and arranging the words with such loving care. They are called "words of truth" *and* "words of delight."

Ecclesiastes also reminds us that much knowledge and many books in themselves are not the point! In these days of the internet, we can easily be fooled. Many words of many websites often lead to weariness rather than the truth or delight we're pursuing.

I recall so wanting our first child to learn to read that, before he was two, I taped up word flash cards all over the house. Fortunately, both God and our children are very forgiving.

May we pray for wisdom as we teach delight in words, beginning with the God-breathed treasures of God's Word.

For Delight in Books and Learning

That you made us to speak to you in words,
O God who spoke and there was light,
is marvelous indeed.
That we can read your Word,
breathed out by you and written down
with study, care, delight,
is wonderful indeed.

I pray that you would help me teach my child
delight in words—your words, all first and foremost,
but as well the words we humans speak and read and write
because we're made by you.

So, as I read aloud, and lead my child to read,
please let us savor words,
with all their rhythms, sounds, and meanings;
may we taste and learn and grow.
May I never make the work an empty labor,
only a weariness of the flesh,
lacking wonder at the gift of words
and wisdom that can come only from you.

So God created man in his own image,
  in the image of God he created him;
  male and female he created them.

. . . And God saw everything that he had made, and behold,
  it was very good. (Gen. 1:27, 31)

The goodness of two distinct, God-ordained genders is a radical and often unpopular concept these days. How we need to hear the beautiful truth of God's Word on these matters, and how we must show and teach our children to love and live this truth!

This prayer asks God to help us to this end both at home and in the church; in both contexts, he shows the beauty of his created order in the distinction and the unity of women and men who love and serve him together according to his plan.

May the Lord give us relentless commitment to his Word and strength to pass on the Word's truth with clarity and joy.

Heirs together of the grace of life: see 1 Peter 3:7.

For Finding Male and Female Very Good

Let her early see at home and in your family, Father God,
a beautiful array of male and female—
fathers, mothers, brothers, sisters, uncles, aunts—
all made by you to live as men and women
in your plan that from creation has been very good.

Let her see your image shining irrepressible
in a man and in a woman—
coming into focus as your Son shines forth
your image through his presence, by his Spirit,
in the new-created ones who trust in him by faith,
male and female, heirs together of the grace of life.

Keep me, Father, from defining male and female
simply as I wish, or listening to voices all around;
help me hear and teach your Word with clarity,
celebrate your sovereign hand,
and model your design
with faithfulness, humility, and joy.

And may my child,
by your good grace,
receive the gift of who she is;
may she find your plan of making human beings
male and female
very good.

If they had been thinking of that land from which they had gone out, they would have had opportunity to return. But as it is, they desire a better country, that is, a heavenly one. Therefore God is not ashamed to be called their God, for he has prepared for them a city. (Heb. 11:15–16)

We want our children to love home. All of us human beings have an instinct to cherish the comfort, the safety, and the belonging that a home represents. We do our best to give the gift of home to our children, as God allows us, and we take joy in doing so.

And yet we know—and it is good to know—that this instinct for home points us far ahead to the home for which we were created, a home without sin where we will dwell together with God's family in God's very presence, only by his grace to us in the Lord Jesus. As we relish the gift of our homes and families now, imperfect as they are, may we pray for eyes to look ahead, and plan ahead, for our forever home with the Lord.

For a Healthy Sense of Home

Father, make our home a place of grace and peace;
may my child rest to know he is at home
and loved, accepted, free to speak,
and hearing voices making harmony, not discord.

May my child embrace the place of home
and love to feel our home stretch
as we embrace new faces coming in
to join a family circle
whose dimensions you decide.

May my child, in loving home,
be learning longing for a better home,
the one for which we're made,
a home with you,
in your full presence—
in that city you prepare for us
and that we long to see.

As I make home with this dear child,
please teach him (and teach me)
to relish this good place with open hands
and open hearts; grow in us, Lord,
a deep desire for our heavenly home.

Now the LORD said to Abram, "Go from your country and your kindred and your father's house to the land that I will show you. And I will make of you a great nation, and I will bless you and make your name great, so that you will be a blessing. I will bless those who bless you, and him who dishonors you I will curse, and in you all the families of the earth shall be blessed." (Gen. 12:1–3)

How do we teach our little children about the whole big world out there? Little by little. Books and songs and people— especially people—can help us.

My father taught at a seminary attended by students from all over the globe; they often joined us for meals, bringing with them all sorts of stories about places far away. Sometimes my sister and I would be bored, sitting there in the midst of the adult conversation. But, looking back, I realize that a lot of that conversation seeped into our thinking and opened up our minds to God's work across the world.

Even as we must focus on the details of here and now, as we care for a child, we can pray to teach that child the ways in which God loves the whole world he made.

For a Heart That Stretches round the Globe

From my child's earliest days, O Father God,
would you help me give her glimpses
clear and hopeful, of a whole wide world
all made and loved by you?

From my child's youngest years,
may our church family help her see
not just the beauty of your body here and now,
but also, Christ our Lord,
the wonder of your body growing,
singing praises with a thousand tongues
so different from our own,
and stretching far
to bring your promised blessing
even to all the families of the earth.

From my child's youth and onward,
may she learn to love your family
with open heart, like yours,
a heart that stretches round the globe.

Blessed are the merciful, for they shall receive mercy.
(Matt. 5:7)

Mercy is probably not a quality we will explain to our child early on—but we'll be acting it out, by God's grace, and teaching it implicitly as we respond with kindness to the needy (including our children), even when they do not seem to "deserve" it.

We'll show mercy imperfectly, but increasingly, by God's grace, as we more and more grasp the great mercy of the Lord toward us sinful human beings who deserve nothing but his wrath.

It often seems that our children follow our heart attitudes even better than they follow our verbal instructions. The heart attitude of mercy is catching. What a prayer: that our children would "catch" mercy from us as we learn it from our heavenly Father.

You are keeping your kind hand: see Psalm 145:9.

For a Heart of Mercy

You are a merciful God and Father;
even when we do not look up,
in your goodness and your mercy
you are keeping your kind hand
over all that you have made.
Your mercy in Christ covers your children;
you've pitied us and drawn us, saved us
through your Son, when we deserve
the wages of our sin.

Grant me, I pray, a heart of mercy;
let me show my child your heart.
Please grow in him, O Lord of mercy,
a heart like yours for those around—
for a needy or bothersome neighbor or friend,
or one who's hurt, or hard.

Give my child eyes to see a needy soul
beneath a prickly surface
that would seem to turn all help away.
Let him not answer hurt with hurt;
let him pursue, and love,
and lend a human hand
that shows a heavenly mercy.

For the LORD your God is God of gods and Lord of lords, the great, the mighty, and the awesome God, who is not partial and takes no bribe. He executes justice for the fatherless and the widow, and loves the sojourner, giving him food and clothing. (Deut. 10:17–18)

This prayer asks for understanding of justice even as we pray to instill a love of justice in our children. Our understanding of justice begins with Genesis's teaching that God created human beings in his image, and it is rooted in his law that reflects his perfect truth and goodness. We see justice fully only in Jesus, who lived God's law perfectly and died to suffer the punishment of those who couldn't.

These are large concepts, ones we can flesh out in our interactions with the people around us—perhaps with children who have been threatened or mistreated, or women who have suffered abuse, or people without a home. Some of my friends' children are learning justice as their families care lovingly for foster children. Our homes are natural places to practice justice and teach it to our children as we show hospitality and invest in relationships with fatherless and widows and sojourners of all sorts.

These are the ones, Deuteronomy tells us, for whom the Lord executes justice. These are the ones we his people can look for as we pray to live out and pass on the kind of justice that reflects our God.

For Love of Justice

How do I pray for love of justice, Lord?
I pray for love of you,
for only you are just—
and only by your mercy
do we live and move
and sing your praise,
our perfectly just and merciful Lord.

From youngest days, may my child hear
a melody of justice
ringing loud in all the songs our family sings
from day to day,
a melody that lifts up every girl and boy
and woman and man,
each made in the image of God,
each needing family love
and food and clothes
and work to learn and do
and laws that do not lie—
and most of all the love of God
who shows his justice and his mercy at the cross.

In our world discordant with injustice,
may this child learn to sing your justice, Father God;
may she grow to love and live your justice,
following your Son.

When I am afraid,
I put my trust in you. (Ps. 56:3)

We will not pray that our children will never fear, because of course they will, and often—and so will we.

But we can teach them what to do with their fears and where to go: to the Lord God who often tells us not to fear, for we can put our trust in him. There is no psychological answer to the problem of fear, but there is One who is greater than our fears.

There is no other place to go with our fears but to the Lord himself. He is awesome and to be feared; but in his love and in his presence, our fears are stilled.

Actually, a peaceful child whose nighttime crying we have comforted can teach us much about the answer to our fears.

For a Fearful Child

Meet my child in his fears, O loving Lord;
please help him learn to trust in you
before he even knows or speaks your name.
Be near him;
let him know that you are here.

When it is nighttime, dark,
or when a young imagination
fears a scary something threatening
or the unknown looming . . .

Help him to grow in trust along with years;
may he not give himself to fear—
not throwing proper fear away,
that fear of you,
an awesome God who speaks,
but turning from the voices
that would call him
not to trust or to obey.

May my voice speak and may he hear
the name of Jesus,
your beloved Son who came
to dwell with us, our Savior, ever near.

May my child, in his fears,
learn early how to put his trust
in you.

To you I lift up my eyes,
  O you who are enthroned in the heavens! (Ps. 123:1)

The reality of heaven and all the hosts of heaven that are invisible to us right now comes better into focus, somehow, in the presence of a child. Perhaps that's because children have a natural capacity to imagine things they cannot see.

How important, then, to teach them early about heaven, especially when they ask (which they tend to do). And how important to fill their minds not just with general imaginings and conjectures but rather with the riches of the Word. The Bible points ahead vividly, and it tells us all we need to know in order to imagine in good and godly ways.

Let's talk with our children about heaven, and let's pray to do it in a way that pleases our Father in heaven.

For a Child Who Asks about Heaven

Lord, give me words
when my child asks
about the things we cannot see,
especially things above
where you sit on your throne—
and Jesus there at your right hand.

Please make my words both deep and true,
according to your Word,
that I might speak into the depths
of a child's mind and heart,
so open and prepared
to trust and to imagine with delight
the brilliant, perfect truth of heaven,
right there, as through an open door—
if we could see.

Help my words show the ground of faith
(of seeing what's invisible)
on which my child's life will build,
so when she grows
into the cares of overseeing
all the daily stuff we see,
she'll not forget to lift her eyes
to the realities above—
to you who reign in heaven.

But we do not want you to be uninformed, brothers, about those who are asleep, that you may not grieve as others do who have no hope. (1 Thess. 4:13)

Many a person's story hearkens back to an early memory of a close encounter with death. We humans are shaken by this enemy, death. But we humans, including our young ones, can grieve with faith and hope as we learn the realities of heaven and as we come to know and trust the Lord Jesus who died for us and rose from the dead.

God himself will sustain his people, including his youngest ones, by the power of his Son who conquered death forever. Let's pray to that end.

For a Child Grieving a Death

Lord, I would want to keep my child
from seeing how death keeps reaching in
to steal this life, and that one—
not just old, but young,
and not just sick and dying,
but alive and in the midst of carrying on
and suddenly snuffed out.

I pray that you would help me show
how we are called to live
right now in company with death,
which tells us of our sin—
but tells us even more of Jesus,
your own Son who came and died
and conquered sin and death
upon that cross,
who rose in triumph from the grave.

So, Lord, please help me teach my child to grieve,
to sorrow, to lament the awfulness of death,
but not to grieve as others do,
who have no hope.
How grief and hope share space
in human hearts
we learn by faith along the way.
Help me both learn and teach, I pray,
as my child sees and grieves a death.

Discretion will watch over you,
understanding will guard you. (Prov. 2:11)

This prayer hardly needs commentary—and, of course, such prayers will grow as our children grow. The effect of technology on the lives of even little children is as huge as its effect in every other stage of life. My five-year-old granddaughter can find my digital photos and do things with them that I could never imagine.

To pray about these matters from the start will, by God's grace, help set our hearts to acknowledge humbly our great need for his wisdom and help, even as we enjoy the great benefits and pleasures of the amazing virtual world.

For My Child in a World of Technology

Someday, dear Lord, he will be grown
and all alone responsible for every click
on every website, every word and picture
that he reads and sees and sends
for all to witness.

But now, dear Lord, while he is young,
not knowing right hand from the left,
I pray that you would help me know
the weight of every moment's choice
I make for him
of words, of pictures,
of an easy slice of entertainment
shaping lifelong inclinations,
memories, affections deep.

I pray for understanding and discretion,
wisdom promised in your Word
and given to overflowing
through the living, present Christ in me.
Let that wisdom rule our home
as we choose images and words to welcome in.
Let me listen humbly
to your Scriptures and your saints,
not ever casually,
and not presuming on my store of wisdom
or the stores of others
not attuned to hear your voice.

I thank you, Lord, for wisdom that is ours in Christ.

So, whether you eat or drink, or whatever you do, do all to the glory of God. (1 Cor. 10:31)

One of our children used to hold a bite of food in his mouth, if he didn't like it, and refuse to swallow. He could do it for hours.

As we came to realize, this was not a major battle—only an extremely minor one. But dealing with food in one way or another takes up a great deal of our waking moments, especially as we raise young children; it is worth asking what God means for us to learn (and to teach) in regard to our eating practices.

We can revel in the confidence that God created us and cares about us as bodily creatures, made to eat and drink regularly—and to his glory.

For Good Eating

We always thank you for our food, our Father God,
but here I am to ask you for your help
to make our eating good,
not just in joyful times of being there
together, face to face—
or sometimes simply quiet times—
but also in our taking of the food
and eating . . .

Would you grow my child's delight in food provided
(both the ordinary and the more uncommon)?
Would you even from the youngest age
help her take pleasure in a satisfying meal
(while learning how to wait for the right time)?
Would you lead her to connect
all good provision with your bountiful providence
(never grasping but receiving humbly from your hand)?

The way you made us, Lord,
makes us spend time, large portions of our days,
in planning and procuring and preparing—
and then *eating* food we need
to live and grow to serve you.
Amid applesauce and oats and peas,
in times of plenty and in times of want,
please let us young and old together
learn to eat and savor daily bread
with truly thankful hearts
and in the name of Jesus who gives life,
the bread of life that lasts forever.

In the beginning, God created the heavens and the earth. (Gen. 1:1)

That children like to make things we all know; seeing their creative instinct from the beginning is one of the happiest parts of raising children. As their creativity develops, our parent role is large at the start and gradually decreases. Our role as pray-ers, though, never ceases.

It is fitting for us to thank the Maker of all things for this part of his image in us and in our children—and to ask that he would help us encourage our young children joyfully and wisely as they learn to make things and to give honor to the Lord in their making.

Through whom and for whom: see Colossians 1:16.

For the Joy of Making Things

From the delight of shaping lips
to make a certain sound,
to the accomplishment of stacking wooden blocks
into a tippy tottering tower,
to the astonishing abstract art
of colors swirled and zigzagged on a page,
to words combined to mean what he intends to mean . . .
let my child love to learn to make things, Lord,
and let his making give you glory,
you who made all things and called them good.

Help me wait to let my child create, I pray—
not regularly rushing in to move on, tidy, fix,
but seeing him learn how to be a little maker
in the image of the One who made him,
taking time to grasp just how he likes to make
and praying to encourage all the gifts
bound up in this young image-bearer.

Let him reflect your image, Father,
as he comes to know and trust your Son.
In all my child's making, let him honor Jesus,
through whom and for whom everything was made.
I pray for joy in making things
all his life long—and for your glory alone.

Now [David] was ruddy and had beautiful eyes and was handsome. (1 Sam. 16:12)

That little hint of physical beauty in David the young shepherd boy has always intrigued me: he had beautiful eyes! Abraham's wife Sarah was called beautiful, as were Abigail and Tamar and Abishag and Esther (see Gen. 12:11–14; 1 Sam. 25:3; 2 Sam. 13:1; 1 Kings 1:4; Est. 2:7).

It is sometimes hard for us to judge just what is beautiful and why, but there is no doubt that God creates beauty all around us and means for us to enjoy it in a way that honors and acknowledges him. We even get to make beauty ourselves as we reflect the image of our Creator. How good to pray that we (and our children) will celebrate beauty with God's eyes and for his glory.

For Love of Beauty

O Lord, I know that outward beauty is not all—
the beauty of a face, a tree, a song—
but you through beauty show yourself,
and pierce a human heart.
So, as I pray my child will love what's beautiful,
I'm praying for her heart to long for you
as she encounters beauty you've so prodigally given,
and for her heart to feel the sadness
of that beauty being spoiled—
in a hateful face or song,
a tree diseased,
a body broken.

Please show me how to fill her life with hints
of beauty showing off your heart—
in a flower we admire,
a vase that's elegantly shaped,
an athlete with a graceful step,
a melody we hum with pleasure,
a smile that makes us smile.

Make her susceptible to beauty, Lord,
so she will stop and see
and see more deeply in
to what you've made and who you are.

May all the hints,
illumined by your Word,
show her the beauty, Lord, of you.

But godliness with contentment is great gain, for we brought nothing into the world, and we cannot take anything out of the world. But if we have food and clothing, with these we will be content. (1 Tim. 6:6–8)

It seems like many people write and talk a lot about contentment these days; ironically, many of us who have been given much are ones who struggle to be content with what we have been given. We so often want more.

Contentment is a close cousin to joy; these qualities overflow from knowing God and being in his presence with his people. Joy and contentment can flow from one person to another; this is especially beautiful in a family setting when children begin to learn these good qualities from the overflow of parents who exemplify "godliness with contentment."

With God's help, we can teach children what to want. And we can pray that they would want more and more of our God who pours out infinite love and unending joy through his Son.

For Contentment

If I could draw a picture of contentment, Lord,
that picture would be of a child
who's fed and clean and loved
and sleeping soundly, breathing deeply,
quiet, utterly at rest.

I pray that simple, deep contentment
might long linger in our home.
As clothes and toys and friends
may quickly, happily multiply,
please give us quiet hearts,
both young and old,
delighting in what's daily given,
much or little,
reaching out with joy
but never grasping tight
or longing with a bitter soul.

In sum, Lord, please help all those in this home
to seek and find our joy in you,
our full contentment in your full provision
of eternal life that never ends,
abundant life right now,
and rest, sweet rest of body and of soul,
all through the saving love
of Christ our Lord.

Children, obey your parents in the Lord, for this is right. "Honor your father and mother" (this is the first commandment with a promise), "that it may go well with you and that you may live long in the land." Fathers, do not provoke your children to anger, but bring them up in the discipline and instruction of the Lord. (Eph. 6:1–4)

I know: this is the second prayer about obedience. But can we ever have too many of them?

Probably not. Obedience is God's primary, repeated command to children—and so follows parents' primary responsibility to teach children to obey. It's huge. It's challenging. It's also full of grace, especially as we keep falling on our knees before our heavenly Father and asking for his help.

God gives help generously when we ask. Out of the abundant love of the three-personed Godhead, we are given grace to teach the obedience that we could never achieve ourselves but that God's Son achieved on our behalf. Let's teach that.

For Honoring and Obeying

To honor and obey, Lord—
teach him.
Teach me, I pray.
And may the love of God the Father of us all
shine unmistakably on us
as by his Word and through his Spirit
we know perfect Father-love.
O heavenly Father, let us honor and obey you,
child and parent alike, within this home.

To honor and obey, Lord—
shape his heart.
Shape mine, I humbly pray.
And may our home be full
of words and thoughts and love
all flowing toward the Son
who came to do his Father's will
and died for us who miss the mark
of full obedience to you our holy God.

To honor and obey, Lord—
bend his will.
Bend mine, I pray. Work in us, by your Spirit.
When my loved child would turn and disobey—
from littlest rebellion on,
whether it be touching a forbidden something
or saying no and trying out the voice of disrespect—
may he be one who stops and listens to my voice
and by your Spirit bends his will to mine
and finally to yours, all his life long.

When pride comes, then comes disgrace,
   but with the humble is wisdom. (Prov. 11:2)

Whoever humbles himself like this child is the greatest in the
kingdom of heaven. (Matt. 18:4)

How do we pray for humility in our children? The world would
tell us to spend more time praying for them to be happy and
secure in their own identity.

The world would tell only part of our story—and so it's not
the true story. God's Word starts with creation, a beginning that
puts us in our place as beings with no life in ourselves until it is
given to us . . . but loved by a Creator who gives life to us! The
Bible doesn't leave out the fall, the story's ultimately humbling
crisis. But then comes the promise of redemption, and finally
the coming of God's own Son to save us—and ultimately the
promise of his coming again to make all things new.

Scripture's full story lights up our utterly needy position
before our God—and our full security in trusting Christ's saving work for us. What beautifully humbling truths, truths good
for children at all stages.

For Humility

You've put us in a school, we parents,
where the lesson for today, if we receive it,
drives down deep the theme of helplessness—
a child's utter need for sustenance
from someone greater than herself,
if she would live.

So help me as your child to help my child, I pray,
with strength and wisdom all from you.
Help me to teach my child to love that place secure
where one has learned to receive help from heaven.
Would you by grace lead her to find her way
courageously, creatively—
and always humbly,
open to hear wisdom's voice
that comes from you, O Lord,
poured out from your own mouth for all your children.

As my child grows, keep her from pride,
from letting her own voice be loudest;
help me to help her moderate her voice
to make it strong and confident—
and always humble,
happy to give praise
to you who gave your only Son.

And as I teach my child humility, Lord,
help me to learn the lesson well myself,
in this good school we parents all attend.

But we see him who for a little while was made lower than the angels, namely Jesus, crowned with glory and honor because of the suffering of death, so that by the grace of God he might taste death for everyone. (Heb. 2:9)

So many things there are to pray for, along the way! As we walk with our children on the first part of their path, let's fix our eyes on the One who walks with us: the living Lord Jesus. Let's pray for our children to know him and see him. This is the main thing.

This will be the main thing in the end: that we will see Jesus, the one who died for us and who conquered death for us. Let's pray that our children see the end even from the beginning. Let's pray in Jesus's name, and for his glory, to the end.

For My Child to Think on Jesus

In the midst of all our bustling days,
O Lord who knows and sees our bustle,
may we not forget the presence of our Savior.
May my child be learning how to think on him who died for us,
to see him,
as his Spirit opens our eyes.

In the midst of play,
of meals either hurried or prolonged,
in quiet rest and busy running,
may my child be mindful of the risen Christ
right here with us,
as his Word lights our eyes to see.

In the midst of growth,
with needy body that demands much care
and mind that would be filled and satisfied,
may my child think on Jesus,
Lord of all things made by his own hand,
and Lord who lives in us who trust in him.

May my child think on Jesus,
seeing all the rest more clearly
in the light of him.

Likewise the Spirit helps us in our weakness. For we do not know what to pray for as we ought, but the Spirit himself intercedes for us with groanings too deep for words. And he who searches hearts knows what is the mind of the Spirit, because the Spirit intercedes for the saints according to the will of God. (Rom. 8:26–27)

We truly do not know what to pray for as we ought. But the Lord helps us. He helps us in our parenting. He helps us in our prayers. "The Lord is my helper; I will not fear" (Heb. 13:6).

And so we can say "Amen" with faith, confident that our Father God hears us as we come to him in the name of Jesus Christ his Son and in the power of the Holy Spirit who dwells in us.

For My Parent Heart

Lord, it is true:
I do not know the things to pray for as I ought.
For I am weak indeed.
And so I thank you that the Spirit helps your children
in our weakness,
interceding for us with a groaning deep,
too deep for words.

Bringing my few feeble prayers to you, my Father God,
I thank you that you know my heart,
and more—you know what is the mind
of your own Spirit who groans deeply for us,
bringing prayers on our behalf.
And more—the Spirit intercedes for us
with perfect prayers, according to your will.

What comfort, Lord, is here:
that I am helped eternally
in all my little prayers,
and that the Godhead takes my part
when weak I come to you,
but as your child, redeemed by your dear Son,
and in whom lives your Holy Spirit.

In my weakness, then, my God,
in simple faith, I ask
that you would hear my prayers
according to your will
for my beloved child.

Conclusion

While preparing to write a conclusion to this volume of prayers, I received a text message from a friend who works with some Christian schools in Southeast Asia. She requested prayer for a fourth-grade girl in a remote village who had been attending school but who had just been given away in marriage.

Three things struck me as I read that message and then thought about these prayers—first, the privilege to pray for the children God gives us, whether close or far away. As believers, we can bring them to him. God our Father understands our requests. Jesus the Son intercedes for us. The Spirit helps us in our prayers. We can pray. We get to pray for the children.

Second, I was struck by what a dangerous world this is for children. Whether the dangers are near or far, visible or hidden (maybe even lurking behind comfort or progress), children are vulnerable indeed. Dangers, toils, and snares often come early. Children need our prayers.

Third, I was struck by God's grace toward such vulnerable ones—which ultimately means all of us. That Jesus should stop in the midst of his important ministry and call the children to himself (Matt. 19:13–15) tells us of his mercy and grace to all of us needy ones who come to him.

You will have children in your life both near and far for whom you are praying. I hope these prayers serve as an ongoing encouragement to you as you pray. Perhaps in these final blank pages you can write down some of your own prayers for your children. Perhaps you will find ways to join with others who are lifting up children to the Lord.

What grace, that we can pray for children in the name of Jesus.

Prayers of a Parent

Did you enjoy this book?
Consider leaving a review online.
The author appreciates your feedback!

Or write to P&R at editorial@prpbooks.com
with your comments. We'd love to hear from you.